Trucking From Home

5 Ways to Invest and Start A Trucking Business

Cheyara Collier

Trucking From Home: 5 Ways to Invest and Start A Trucking Business

Published by Cheyara Collier

Table of Contents

This book is dedicated to:

I would like to dedicate this book to my favorite girl and best friend my mother Corliss White for her constant motivation and support. Your support has been unwavering and abundant over the years. Raising a child like myself is not easy. You always have encouraged me to dream bigger and dream differently. You always reminded me that it was okay to march to my own beat and to make sure I am doing what I need for me at all times. For this reason, I am forever grateful.

To my father Tony Collier who has always encouraged me and always reminded me that I should not care what people think of me and for the many lessons you have taught me over the years I am forever grateful.

To my friend and mentor Taurea Avant for being the inspiration for me to start writing to help grow my business. You are the epitome of never giving up. Thank you! Thank you! Thank you!

I also would like to thank all of my friends that have reached out to me with a word of encouragement. You are supportive beyond words and it is forever appreciated.

Romans 13:8
Let no debt remain outstanding, except the continuing debt to love one another, for whoever loves others has fulfilled the law.

<u>Acknowledgments</u>

Thank you to the first supporters of my first

book. I am forever appreciative of your

continued support! You are simply amazing.

Thank you! Thank You! Thank You!

Chelsia McCoy
Cassandra Mouton
Janeisha Scharkley
Mia Sumpter
Corliss White
Angela Williams

INTRODUCTION

As I sit at my computer trying to figure out exactly what it is that I feel this industry could give to you I am at a loss for words. Not because I do not know what to say but because there is just so much to tell. Had I known what I know now, back when I was in my early twenties and fresh out of high school, I would have made a lot of different decisions. As a young adult, we think we know everything and are invincible. In hindsight, I would have made a lot of different decisions had I had the guidance and the right people around me.

What I've learned over the past few years is that your success is a direct reflection of your surroundings. I would have positioned myself to be around more positive people and more ambitious people than the people I was already around. The people I was around in college are amazing however, I would have made sure I networked better, I would have been intentional about meeting more that looked different than myself and I definitely would have found a mentor early on. Now granted when I went to college everyone was doing one thing but truthfully none of us had it figured out. It is so common nowadays for us to go to college, spend all this money are getting educated in the areas that we think that we are going to go into, and then end up going in a completely different direction as soon as you graduate. We have to pay the bills so sometimes our jobs are dictated by the necessity to survive.

When I started college, I thought I knew what I wanted to do and within the first semester, I realized I really didn't know. Originally, I was going to major in Communication at Middle Tennessee State

University, causing my first semester of college to not be as successful as it should have been because I was taking the wrong classes and had the wrong focus. But looking back on it now, my life experiences have carried me further than my college education. I am not saying that education is not valuable but it is costly. Most of my close friends are not working in the field in which they received their degree. One thing that we all have in common is the fact that we have student loans. Had I known more about entrepreneurship in the logistics industry I may not have even gone to college at all because this field is much more lucrative than several of the jobs that I had after college graduation.

Please interpret this correctly -- I am **not** telling you to avoid going to college because there were a lot of things that I did learn in college. But what I **am** saying is that sometimes life experiences can be more valuable to your circumstances and your future plans compared to only having the books. When I completed college, I had a Bachelor of Science in General Studies. To some extent, I guess you could consider my degree still falling in the field that I work in but it was not my initial goal when I went to college. I really finished college to complete the task and earn my degree. Graduating from college was very important to me because it meant breaking the generational curse of others in my family who did not finish college or even attend. It also meant I would increase my chances of being able to be promoted on my job as well. So, yes, my goal of graduating college was not just for me but for the legacy I am leaving to those coming up behind me.

What inspired me to write this book is to let people know about another opportunity and another way to make more money. Have you ever thought about what your next plan would be if your job fired you today? Unemployment is not going to cover the bills. You only get so many weeks of getting those benefits. You must have a backup plan if you want to ensure your stability. Even if you do not decide to go into the logistics or the transportation industry after you read this book, I hope you will at least consider becoming an entrepreneur in some form or fashion. Entrepreneurship is a lifeline. You do not have to be a full-time entrepreneur but you do need multiple streams of income. The path on how you get there is up to you but I'm just showing you the path that I chose. The recession of the early 2000's was not that long ago. Recessions take jobs and homes away which remove stability away from you and your family if that is the only source of income that you are relying on.

As this book is finishing its final editing stages this entire world is experiencing job interruptions and life interruptions that were never expected due to the Coronavirus-19. People have lost jobs, been laid off their jobs and/or having to reduce their work hours because the government has mandated that people stay home to prevent the spread of the virus. This type of thing is worse than a recession because it has affected the entire world – not just the United States. How many of us were prepared for this type of thing? I have been affected as well because my income has had stopped completely. Being an entrepreneur with multiple streams of income is even more critical now than ever. In addition, next year will be 2021. It is time to change the things that we do not like, it is time to build wealth for our future, and it's time to accomplish the goals that we could only dream about. Being financially stable opens so many doors and opportunities that you never probably would have considered. It is time to position yourself for greatness and allow yourself to have more options.

I was also inspired to encourage more minorities and young adults to get involved in this industry. With the right guidance and mentor, you could make more money in this industry without college than it costs to go to college within a year. I am not saying this industry is easy but there is a lot of potential for anyone in this industry. You can create a significant amount of generational wealth with the right game plan. Generational wealth is so important. Do not be the person that does not leave anything for their grandchildren.

This book is for anyone who is curious about the logistics and transportation industry. This book is also for the person who is a serial entrepreneur and looking for another way to invest their money and make it work for them. This book will help with the idea for your next chapter in life if you are serious about taking this information to help you move forward. There are multiple ways to get into the transportation industry and not necessarily drive a truck. That is something I learned on my journey into the logistics industry and I'm so glad I found it.

After reading this book, I hope you can find and identify a way in which you can be involved in this industry. The transportation industry is a trillion-dollar industry and it is just as good of an industry to be involved with as real estate. The transportation industry is not going anywhere. Whether we are in a recession or not in a recession goods will need to be moved. There are a lot of similarities that you can find between the two industries when it comes to return on investment. You can be an active participant in this industry or you could be a passive participant in this industry. The way that you get to your money is up to you because there are so many paths that you can follow and there's not just one way that will work for everyone. I hope by the end of this book you can identify which way may be a good fit for you. All of the areas that you can make money that I will discuss in this book you can start from home. It's up to you if you decide to get an office space or work somewhere outside of your home. It's up to you to implement some of the ideas that I put in this book.

1

Becoming an Entrepreneur

Becoming an entrepreneur is not for everyone but I do feel it could be one of the best things you can do for yourself when planning your financial future. Entrepreneurship is a lot of work but it can be very satisfying at the same time. Mainly, because you know at the end of the day you are working for yourself and you are reaching personal goals. You have to determine if entrepreneurship is the right path for you because it will be one of the most difficult tasks you will undertake in your life if you are trying to be successful. You also have to look at how much flexibility as an entrepreneur that you do have. It will require a lot of discipline.

The truth of the matter is the days of working for one company for 30 years and expecting a pension is over. Preparing for a financial future is viral at a younger age as opposed to our grandparents. Fortune 500 companies in many small businesses are not loyal to the employees that they have. It's more about who you know versus what you know and if you don't know the right person you might be stuck in the same position for a lot longer than you have hoped to be. So starting a business allows you to work in the interest that you love and also if you handle your phone's correctly allows you a lot of benefit tax-wise, also allows you to prepare for your retirement in a different capacity then your job, and you can set yourself in a can be financially well-off based off of doing a few years of hard work for your stuff versus doing

Decades of word for another company to make them richer. Many entrepreneurs understand that building wealth is important not only for ourselves before our children to be able to have the best that we can offer them.

The truth about starting a business is that it will require you to relearn or learn new ways to accomplish tasks. You can always source things out to other people to complete but it will affect your bottom line. When you are just starting in your business, I highly recommend sourcing out activities that are not your strong points. For example, when I started my business I completed all of my paperwork to start my business and set up a business checking account. You still need logos, email addresses, accounting systems, websites, etc. to be completed to become a legit business presence online. If you have the money to have someone do this for you then no problem. However, if you are just starting this is something you should consider.

If you pay attention to the patterns in our economy today Mini businesses are closing left and right. You can look at Macy's, Payless Shoes, Bed Bath & Beyond, and Sears to see that major corporations are closing down because the importance of having a brick-and-mortar business is not there anymore. A lot of smaller online retailers as well as larger online retailers are putting a lot of these brick-and-mortar businesses out of business. at one point in time, it was important for users to be able to go into a store and purchase items that you need it. But places like Amazon Prime and walmart.com have made it so easy to avoid having to do in-person shopping.

Being a laptop entrepreneur is becoming more common. So do not worried about trying to have a brick-and-mortar place and less the type of business you run is required to have a brick-and-mortar storefront to have a business. The ways that you can start a business in my book are businesses you really can start from home. Having a storefront is optional in the line of work that we do. You also have alternative workspaces so just co-working spaces. These are great but the only downfall is that if you have a fleet of trucks you will need to find a place to park these trucks outside of the co-working spaces.

     I have put together a free business start-up to help you set up businesses with these discount codes. You can get this by texting the word **"Free99"** to **31996**. I hope you find it helpful. My goal is to help you start your business without spending a lot of money.

     The one thing that will not be going anywhere is the transportation industry. All online retailers utilize trucking of some sort to transport their goods from one side of the country to the other. Amazon has Sprinter vans, 18-wheeler trucks, aircraft, and use other services such as UPS who also has trucks to get items to consumers in a very quick manner. These are just a couple examples of how you can invest in the trucking industry or either work in the trucking industry and make a large profit because the industry is here to stay.

2

Why You Should Consider Starting a Trucking Business or Investing in the Trucking Industry

There are several reasons to get into Transportation and Logistics Industry. Below are 10 reasons, then you can decide for yourself if it's a good fit for you.

1. It's a BILLION-dollar industry and trucking moves 71% of all freight in America[1]. It's not the **easiest** industry to be in but it's not hard to make money

---

[1] "11 Incredible Facts about the $700 billion trucking industry. Steven John, 2019. Retrieved from: https://markets.businessinsider.com/news/stocks/trucking-industry-facts-us-truckers-2019-5-1028248577

if you have a carefully strategized game plan. There is money to be made everywhere you just have to decide on exactly what role you want to play in figuring out how to make money doing it.

2. E-commerce: Online shopping has become the biggest way a lot of people shop today. Do you realize how much money major retailers make throughout the year and during the Christmas season? The Christmas season is such a lucrative time to have trucks on the road. People are moving everything everywhere during this time of year. Whether you're buying stuff online or shipping it to a family member in a different area of the country trucks are going to be moving.

3. Your business can grow significantly in multiple ways with a business in the

transportation and logistics industry. You don't have to be on the road. You do not have to be stuck behind a computer. You can be the manufacturer, retailer, truck dealer, dump truck, etc. There are so many opportunities to make money in this industry that could set up your future. It's ridiculous.

4. Trucking/logistics is not going anywhere. People are always going to need something moved/delivered from point A to point B no matter what the item is. Trucking is the primary way we transport things across this country. Yes, we have ships, airplanes, and trains but trucks are the most common and sometimes the most cost efficient.

5. This industry is just as good to invest in as real estate. The market does fluctuate however you see the same or close to the

same Returns on investment as you do in real estate and freight industry.

6. Your earning potential is Limitless. it comes down to how you stretch your business and your marketing strategy. And even if you do not have a business where you need to market heavy you're still going to make money regardless if you have a huge marketing team or not. Your Potential to earn is as large as your hustle. The person that works harder than the next person will be more successful.

7. Running a trucking business can be done from anywhere. You confirm your loads, you can broker loads, you can track your loads, and manage your employees from a distance. Depending on how comfortable you are with running your business you really could

do everything from your laptop and cell phone.

8. It is easy to get trained and whichever area you decide to branch off into the trucking industry in. there is no degree required to be successful in the transportation industry. You could make a lot of money without having to stay in school long-term. Most training can be done within a few weeks for many of the job roles in this industry.

9. If you decide to start a fleet you don't necessarily have to do it independently you can run a flea under another major carrier which gives you some added support.

10. There's always room to create partnerships with major companies and small carriers. You can put your tracking Fleet under Major Brands like Walmart, Amazon, Landstar Etc. you do not have

to completely start a whole brand independent of the company that you're serving to be successful.

With the trucking industry, you just have to decide what plan is going to work for you. it will take a substantial amount of research for you to determine what fits your personality. But you can be successful in any aspect of the trucking industry. It's not a hard concept to grasp you just have to find your footing. the trucking business is something you can start right out of high school. As with any industry, there are some cons and there are not all pros to the transportation industry.

Some of the drawbacks with this industry is that a can be fickle and very much volatile like the stock market. 2018 was a fantastic year for mini-trucking companies and trucking rates were better than they had ever been before. However, due to the the fast growth of the industry in 2018, the competition and saturation in the market between major and small carriers a lot of companies went out of business or had massive layoffs. You can avoid some of these issues by being strategic and having slow and steady growth. In this case, I would have suggested diversifying how you spend your money in the industry. But that's a story for another time.

3

How Money Is Made in the Freight Industry

For independent businesses in the trucking industry, there are a couple of different paths you can take to make great money. There are multiple roles that people play in moving Freight independently in this industry. You have who helps map out how the truck should run to be the most efficient for their business. There's the broker who negotiates rates with major companies and manufacturers move their goods from one side of the country to the other. You also have owner-operator truck driver who may own a truck or two that makes their money is based on the loads that they receive off of major load boards, or from an independent dispatcher or broker. Fleet owners normally have their trucks contracted with several businesses and manufacturers to move their freight for them or they use load boards to pick their freight for their drivers. I will give you an idea of how money is made in the trucking industry as an owner-operator of your own business.

What is the load board? load bored our website that has a magnitude of pray that needs to be shipped. Most credible load boards require a paid membership to see what's available. Load boards are websites where brokers put the information somewhere they have freight needing to be shipped. load boards are normally worn you can find the cost that's being offered by the broker to ship their goods. For example, if I had a truck in St Louis Missouri that needed to go to Atlanta

Georgia as a broker I would put all of the information that is required to move this load as well as what I'm willing to pay for this load.

For example, I'm willing to pay $750 for a particular load. After posting the information for the load that I need to ship on one of these load boards I would then get phone calls from truck drivers that own their equipment in business or I will get phone calls from the statues that are trying to plan loads for other Truckers. If my price is fair for the load they will accept the price automatically. If my price is a bit lower then they will try to negotiate my right a little bit higher. From a dispatcher and trucker standpoint it's beneficial to negotiate higher to profit from moving the goods on their track. so likely I'm offering $750 and it cost them $500 to move the product it would be beneficial to negotiate a rate of $900.

As a broker, I have negotiated with the company that I'm moving the freight for at a rate of $1,100 I have a truck driver move their product from one place to another. If I negotiate with a driver or dispatcher to move the freight at $900 I will be left with $200 profit for that day. Whatever rate that we agree upon the broker makes the difference in between the contracted rate with the manufacturer that they're shipping for and the price they negotiate with the truck driver. The truck driver profits the cost of fuel and overhead cost to run their business and in this situation would profit $400. If they had a dispatcher call on their behalf the dispatcher would make the amount of 5 to 10% of the price of the load. So, in this situation if a dispatcher was charging 10% of the load they would have made $90 just to put the load for the truck driver. This process, once you have gotten used to it from the standpoint of a dispatcher and broker, takes less than an hour. The driver still has to drive to his destination, which may take several hours.

You need to start your fleet to run under another company if you do not want to pay the cost of starting your trucking authority upfront. you can run under another carrier that has their DOT and MC number and still make a great profit. A lot of times you want to choose a carrier that has good relationships which major retailers and manufacturers. You will likely have consistent word the more reliable the carrier is that you choose to run under if you decide to go this route. If you attach your trucks to another carrier you don't have to worry about the overhead price of actually starting an authority which is roughly been estimated at $25,000. Your major carrier will also have a reputation for carrying days which is beneficial to you because more people are willing to work with you. After all, the company has already been established for some time. Whereas, if you were to start your authority it would take time for major companies and brokers to trust you with their products to be transported.

No matter how you decide to start your fleet, know that when it comes to how truckers and fleet owners make their money it is very similar. You have to subtract your cost of running a truck and maintaining your Authority or being on a major carrier from the amount of the loads you are receiving. If you are attached to someone else's Authority you will have to pay that company a percentage to be able to run under their MC number and their number. The reason why they charge a percentage is to cover insurance and tax license plate numbers, etc on your behalf. If you are an independent authority you assume all this cost. You will need to consider that when selecting loads for your trucking fleet.

It is very common for truck company owners to process roughly about $10,000 a month from each truck that is on the road. They gross much more; however you have to factor in maintenance, fuel, dispatch fees, employee salaries, and other associated overhead expenses. And profiting $10,000 a month is on a good month where there are not a significant amount of issues going on with your truck. If you have to get any type of truck maintenance this price will decrease.

 I hope I have given you a generalized idea of how money is being made in the trucking industry. If you want more detail on any aspect of this please feel free to reach out to me for a consultation. I'll be glad to talk to you more about what the path may be best for you.

4

Investing Transportation vs. Real Estate

When trying to make money and growing your money by investing, many people turn to real estate or in the trucking industry. Honestly, I think you should invest based on your goals. There are risks that you should consider when investing in either industry but there is a lot of reward and both Industries as well. Here are a few things I feel that you should think about before you decide which path you will take.

Real estate money comes a little bit slower than the money you can make with having your fleet of trucks. If you're looking from the first practice of owning trucks you can average anywhere from five to ten thousand per month with one truck. The variables will be the cost of maintenance, fuel, the type of driver you have in the truck, and other overhead expenses. It will also make a difference if you own your own Trucking Authority versus having your trucking being carried under someone else's Trucking Authority. There is normally a percentage that you must pay to another trucking company if you decide to put your truck under their company.

Depending on the type of rental property or investment property that you plan to flip it may take you an extended period to rent or flip your investment. In the case of actually flipping the property, you have to consider how long it would take you to close on a property, renovate the property, and a length of time that it will take you to sell the property. When it comes to rental properties you have to factor in the cost of maintaining a property, your mortgage, and how many units you have at the location that you are renting.

If you were to rent out a multi-family home with three or more units in the property you would make significantly more in your real estate investment every month where your return is comparable to what someone owning a truck in one month may receive. For instance, if you have a 4-unit property that you spent $150,000 on 4 mortgage payments may be around $1,200 depending on your interest rate. if you have four units and you are charging $900 per unit you will be bringing in $3,600. after you take out the mortgage payment of $1,200 and if there are no maintenance issues you will see a return of reference $2,400 per month. This is an awesome right of return over 12 months. You're looking at nearly $29,000 off of this property if you have no maintenance issues during a year. if you are in a position to have multiple properties that are when real estate is extremely beneficial.

However, if you were to go to a tractor-trailer dealership or auction you could get a decent truck car under $50,000. If you or someone else you hire can stay on the road for weeks at a time and pick really good loads you can easily make $10,000 a month before you take out the cars of running the track. Maintenance issues can be the most expensive part of running trucks outside of fuel costs. For this reason, I would encourage you to invest in building your fleet slowly. The insurance that is required on tractor-trailers is expensive as well. But with the right driver and good upkeep of maintenance, you can earn your monthly overhead within the first week and the other three weeks of the month can be profitable.

The cost of hiring drivers can be an issue as well. Finding a good driver is very hard. The reason why it's so hard is that a lot of drivers know that is not hard to go find another job in the industry that pays better offer more than what you're giving them. You also want to make your business plan structure to where you always are turning a profit even when there are hiccups in the business. Although there is a higher risk of starting a trucking company there is a greater reward.

Just like with real estate you can enter the trucking business without having lots of money. you can start a real estate or a trucking business for less than $1,000 in real estate, you would start with wholesaling property and was tracking. You would either start a dispatching service, become a freight broker agent, or you can start a brokerage. If you decide to start a brokerage it will cost you more than $1,000 just because you have to have a surety bond to start a business independently. However, you can start as a broker agent working under another company's set up and amazing money. Freight broker agents and Freight brokerage companies make their money by taking the difference in the cost of actually moving the freight from the manufacturer to what they negotiate with the truck driver or dispatcher to move the freight. a dispatcher that is independent charges a percentage of the cost to move the freight to the truck driver anywhere from five to 10%. Dispatchers map the most profitable past for their drivers to take to earn more money. Freight dispatchers make the most money by servicing multiple tracks on a fleet or working with multiple owner-operators.

With real estate and trucking industries, you can plan for multiple ways of making income within one idea easily. having a trucking business you can make money dispatching for multiple carriers if you have an authority you can add other trucks on to your authority and charge them a percentage to run under your authority numbers, you can also have a Freight brokerage within your business, etc. Same thing with real estate you can on single-family homes and rent the home out to one family or if you're in a town that has a high volume of college students or is a hub for major airlines you can rent out each room in your home to service those people who do not need a full house to rent. You can also have a multi-family home within your real estate business, you can buy tax liens to add more money coming into your business, you can buy commercial property, etc. both

Industries allow you to grow and expand your business in the way that you see fit.

Both types of businesses succeed and suffer based on what is going on in the economy. Freight lane rates change on a monthly and sometimes daily basis. real estate interest rates and property values are dictated by the demand of housing in the economy and several other factors. Both Industries can be extremely volatile at times.

I would suggest when deciding to invest in either industry that you come in with a plan and being well informed by doing your research. It is very common for people who have businesses in the trucking industry to also have businesses in real estate. Both business types can set you up for a residual income and generational wealth if planned well. Having a trucking business can allow you the capital to invest in real estate very easily, and the profits that you have from real estate can easily help support your growing trucking business.

5

How to Get Started

Research, research, research! I cannot stress this enough when considering starting a business in any industry. What's important to find out about the trucking industry is the trends, your competitors, and the most effective way to set up your business. When researching the trucking industry the first step I would do is, of course, to check and see if you know any owner-operators or just truck drivers, in general, to ask them questions about the type of work they do and what they like and dislike about it. then I will move forward to ask them what aspect of the industry they feel would be smart to get into.

What they dislike about the type of work that you are going to go into.

When I first was considering getting into the industry I consulted my uncle who has been a truck driver all of my life. I was glad to have talked to him about the trucking industry as a whole because he gave me a perspective that I would have never thought of had I not talk to him. He told me different things about what he liked in a good freight dispatcher and what do you like in a freight broker. Both of these areas I was being trained in at the same time. He gave me his opinion on which type of business I should start first but ultimately it was going to be my decision. I've taken his advice and I know I will be transitioning my business at a later time to fit more of my lifestyle needs.

When researching you also want to find the change in the industry. You can go about this in several different ways. There are a plethora of articles that you can research through Google. But you can also look on YouTube and find truck drivers that are doing the same thing that you're interested in doing. I would also recommend that you search out multiple drivers in the trucking industry as well as other people who play a different type of role in the trucking industry. If you do thorough research and listen to what other perspectives have to say you will get a general idea of what is going on in the industry at the time that you decide.

The great thing is the transportation industry is not going anywhere. Major trends like we have to go on recently Coronavirus you can see a good impact on the industry because transportation is needed a lot more because so many businesses have had to limit their service and people require resources. a major epidemic such as the Coronavirus always affects the transportation industry you just have to watch and see if it would be good or bad. Aim Trucking you will notice that there are years that the trucking industry is booming and it's something that everybody should consider getting into and then you have your flight 2019 we're tracking was not so great. Tracking struggled after 2018 because the freight rate for shipping Goods across the country had lowered. In 2018 the market got extremely oversaturated and many trucking companies grew extremely fast when they should have scaled steadily according to how the market was going to grow.

2018 was such a good year for mini-freight companies and trucking companies, and many fleets were adding on several trucks because it was more sustainable to add one truck at a time or two trucks at a time depending on the size of the fleet. In 2019 many truckers ended up having to sell a lot of equipment and there were major layoffs. So in 2020, we have an epidemic that is helping the trucking industry improve in the current moment. There's a lot of money to be made because resources for the American economy is dependent upon the transportation industry more than ever. Truck drivers are important to our economy regularly but the way they get paid changes depending on arms demand.

There are several ways that you can research the trucking industry. One of my favorite websites (they also have a YouTube channel) is called Freight Waves. They have commentary on the industry daily and write articles regularly to keep you posted on what is going on in the transportation world. I would also recommend that you find information through tracking organization websites as well as news articles that are within a year of the date that you're looking at the article. I would highly advise that you pay attention to the last 5 to 10 years of the industry so you can understand how the highs and lows of the transportation business are very volatile. if you understand the trans you can better plan for your business.

The next step is to decide on how you want to be involved in the trucking business. What role is it that you want to play? Do you want a more hands-on approach? Do you want a hands-off approach? Do you NOT want to own a truck? If you do want to own trucks how do you plan to obtain these trucks? Are you going to leave your truck? Are you going to go to an auction?

When I decided on what role I wanted to play in the trucking industry, I did it based off of what my situation was at the time. Honestly, you also have to determine how much money you can financially commit to the start of your business. Many entrepreneurs start-off "bootstrapping" their operations until they gain enough capital to make it a large operation. if this is how you have to start up, by all means, do so. You won't be by yourself. When I started my business that is exactly how I started up. When I did my research, I decided that freight dispatching would be ideal for me. it's a very low overhead business. I started my business in a matter of a week. I did some research on companies that provided training for this type of business and I purchase the training and in my spare time, I began to do the training on my own time. You can receive training for either of these businesses in person or you can do them online. if you do it online you can get the knowledge that you need a lot faster versus waiting on a class to be done. Also doing the courses online digitally is a cheaper way of going about getting the training that you need. a lot of times you will find other people in the industry offering these classes for crazy amounts of money for training. a lot of people will say you will get what you pay for but I also feel that you learn a lot from experience. What you need when you start your business is the basics and the foundation to get started in this business. A lot of people that are offering these courses are charging more than $1,000 to sit in the classroom for 8 hours to show you how to run a trucking business. I am planning to create my own version of these courses that I took and increase the knowledge in areas that I feel that were extremely needed when I first started. Stay tuned!!! The businesses are not hard to start up. I am also providing information towards the end of the book to help you get started.

If you decide to start your trucking fleet, you can do it in several different ways. The key is deciding on what works best for your situation as any business. Some truck drivers start as a truck driver for another major company and save their money to buy their first truck to become an owner-operator. Some people never step a foot into the truck and just purchase them to have them to work under other major carriers.

To be completely hands-free in that type of operation you would have probably want to make sure you have a great freight dispatcher that can handle the administrative side in the back office side of your business, and it will be also great if they can recruit for you to find your truck drivers. I would love to help you in that area and if you have any questions my contact information is in the back of this book. However, there are many businesses out there that can assist you in those areas. You can go about it by working with multiple people and doing everything al a carte. But essentially how to make sure that the person that is over your business can work well with the drivers that you're working with, honest with all business handling, and able to assist you and the ongoing day-to-day tasks of your business. What works for one person does not always work for others. Nonetheless, starting a business is very simple and I have a free guy for you as a gift in the back of my book to assist you with the setup of your business. I have created a guide that can help you start your business and create a brand presence online. that is my gift to you for supporting me by purchasing this book. please feel free to tag me on my page on Instagram and Facebook at Southern Belles Logistics to let me know how you're doing with your business.

6

To Get or Not to Get a CDL?

Is a Commercial Driver's License (CDL) really necessary?

It is not always necessary to have a CDL to have a logistics business but it is very beneficial to your business to have one. Having a CDL can and will be beneficial to someone who has trucks. You can start in this industry as a dispatcher or a broker but if you decide to grow into a fleet, I would strongly consider going through a CDL School before purchasing a truck. When you own a fleet or start your authority with a driver working for you, you have to consider a few things that you may have not thought about.

With a CDL license, you can drive the truck yourself if you so desire but for some people that may not be something, they are interested in doing. When I started my business, Southern Belle Logistics, I knew trucking is not what I personally want to do however, I do have the desire to own a small fleet of trucks. There are many social media influencers that will sell you on the idea of starting your trucking company without having a CDL. A good manager and business owner will know how to do every function within their business. It would be in the best interest of you and your business to obtain the license.

When dealing with truck drivers you are working with a different type of population than you are in most industries than you probably are used to working in. Truck drivers are generally nice people but you may get a temperamental or difficult personality from time to time. It is not uncommon for truckers to abandon trucks and trucking equipment on the side of the road if they are unhappy. If you are a small company and you do not have anyone else to pick up the truck outside of the drivers working for you, you will be at a loss financially. Sometimes you will be the only person available to go pick up the abandoned equipment, and in this situation, this is why you would want to make sure you have a CDL. Truckers know that there are always going to be other companies that will hire them quickly so you will likely deal with a good amount of turnovers until you have built up a great team.

In this business or any business for that matter, you want to be able to have the skill set to not have to rely on someone else. Do not limit yourself on learning the different aspects of logistics, transportation and freight industry. You will never learn everything in this industry but you can become an expert in the area of the industry you specialize in.

My recommendation to anyone unsure about whether a CDL is for them or not I would tell them to figure three things out specifically for the people who have a desire to own a truck or a fleet. The first thing you should figure out is your budget. Do you have the budget to go purchase a truck? If not, how do I plan to go from getting my truck to becoming my own authority or owner-operator? Next, you need to figure out what is the time frame you want to drive. Is this going to be long term or short term? Lastly, this goes for everyone no matter if you plan to drive or not. You need to know your exit strategy or end game in this business. What is your ultimate goal? Knowing this will help you plan according to your goals. Your endgame can be modified as your business goals change but make sure you have a solid idea of what you are trying to do and where you are trying to go in your future. Do not come into this industry and not know your end goal. You could limit your potential growth and money you could be earning. Also, do not put strict deadlines on yourself to hit your target goals. Yes, it is great to do things in the time frame you wish to but being realistic make sure you are giving yourself enough time to get to the next level.

One Last Thing...

If you decide to go for the CDL that is awesome. If you decide it is not for you that is awesome because you did not waste your time or money. For those of you that do get your CDL to make sure you get all of your certifications. You will limit your earning potential. You have to remain compliant in this industry at all times as well. There may be a time you may have to pick up a load that you normally do not carry to make more money. You will limit your risk in being shut down or be fined heavily by getting these certifications. Even though you will be your own boss, you still have to answer to the Department of Transportation (DOT), IFTA Fuel Tax, and Federal Motor Carrier Safety Administration (FMCSA). Whatever you decide at the end of the day make sure it aligns with your vision and goals.

7

How to Make Money as a Truck Driver

Truck driving is one of the most traditional ways that most people come into the transportation industry. Truck driving is seen as a new beginning for most people who come into the industry. Transportation companies hire people who want to start a second career, people with bad credit, people who have criminal records, people with little education and people with a lot of education. This industry can give opportunities to a lot of different kinds of people if you are willing to do research and work hard.

Truck driving is a great and straightforward way to get into the transportation industry. Normally the process is pretty simple to go through however, there are multiple ways to go about working in trucking. The path you choose is really up to you and what is conducive to your lifestyle at the time you start working. The outcome of how successful someone is in trucking comes down to how a person plans their driving schedule, ability to understand the concept of the business and their level of motivation to work in the transportation industry.

There are a few ways to be a truck driver. You can go to a company that will train you on how to drive and you can work for them for a year. This is what a lot of people who have a little start-up money choose to do. You can find a truck driving school self-pay and purchase a truck via cash or leasing. After six months of experience some companies will hire you for Over-The-Road (OTR) driving or regional driving. If you have enough capital you can start your trucking authority and purchase your truck and work for yourself. If you are blessed enough to have the capital to start your trucking authority you will have the option to build your fleet as well.

Types of Trailers

Truck drivers get paid according to the trailer they are pulling. A dry van trailer will not make as much as a "reefer" or refrigerated trailer. Many major carriers have separate divisions for each trailer type that they run. In the back of the book I have a list of different trailer types that are commonly used in the transportation industry. There are several different types of trucks that can be used to start a trucking business. The transportation industry is definitely an industry that is meant for you to decide on what terms you want to be involved in the industry and for you to determine your goals based on your lifestyle.

Getting Your CDL

Depending on the company I have seen people be able to get through CDL school for their licensing in less than three weeks. The most time-consuming part of CDL school is the on the road training that happens right after you get the CDL license. Trucking companies have a set amount of miles or time that is required to be completed with a trainer before you are given the opportunity to get on the road solo. You are driving in teams for a period of about six weeks or however long it takes for you to complete the amount of miles that your company you go with requires.

One thing you want to consider before going into a trucking school is your finances before leaving. If you are in a position to save some money before you enroll in trucking school I would highly suggest you do so. For several of the more popular companies that people sign up with you have to wait a week or two to start getting paid. However, when you start getting paid it will not be the pay you thought you were going to get when you first signed on to work for the company.

The fact is the recruiters lie to get you to sign on with their companies. They are in desperate need to get drivers on the road as soon as possible. Major carriers will let you come in and get your CDL with their company with a year contract. Make sure you are aware of the terms of these contracts you sign, how much you will be making and try to find someone who has worked for the company before. YouTube is a great wealth of information. There are many truck drivers that do videos on these companies and they will be honest about the good, the bad and the ugly of these companies. Do your research before you sign up with a company that does not fit your lifestyle and needs. I included a list of major carriers in the back of the book that you may want to check out. Due to the fact that their websites updated regularly keep up with the industry I highly recommend researching each company thoroughly.

Over-The-Road OTR Driving

Over-The-Road (OTR) driving is how a large percentage of how most people get into the transportation industry. The drivers that do OTR are gone from home for extended periods of time. Typically, when the driver is gone for longer periods of time they tend to make more money if they have good time management skills. In this business you will quickly learn that time is money. The more time you stay on the road the more you make, the faster you get to the destination the quicker you can pick up another load to make more money, essentially how you plan your route is a direct reflection of your income. Most OTR drivers tend to stay on the road a minimum of three weeks at a time. It really depends on their goals and lifestyle on how long they can run.

Regional Driving

Regional drivers are the drivers you see locally. They are able to work and go home daily unless their contract says otherwise. The benefit of coming home every night comes with some cons as well. Some companies with regional require the drivers to assist with unloading the truck on top of driving for them. OTR drivers do not normally assist physically with unloading unless they are removing tarps. Regional drivers normally drive under 2,000 miles weekly where as an OTR driver surpasses that easily. When deciding whether to be OTR or Regional comes down to preference.

Company Driving

Company drivers are the majority of the drivers you see when driving on the freeway or the trucks you see at the stores when you shop. Some company drivers do well but, it depends on how these drivers are hired onto the company as well as many other factors. For instance, how well the company pays its drivers plays a major role in how well a driver potential salary can be. How many years of experience the driver has, will affect their pay grade. The more seasoned drivers tend to do the best. The equipment the driver is pulling makes a huge difference but does not limit their earning potential if the driver knows what they are doing.

The driver's driving schedule is the biggest difference between a five-figure earner and a six-figure earner. How hard they "run" (how long they are out on the road driving) while on the road driving is what this is called. A driver that has one year's experience will make less than a driver that has been driving with a company for several years. Some of the better companies offer bonuses based on how long you drive or how many miles you have driven for a period of time. Team drivers get paid differently depending upon the company. Some people are happy being company drivers and it is a great start for many and a great way to see the country but some truck drivers decide to become their boss due to their ability to earn significantly more than working for a major carrier.

Owner Operator

Owner Operators are their own business and trucking authority. They have their own trucks, they do their own invoicing to the shippers, they work when the feel like it, they are in control of their own business growth and salary. However, they are also responsible for truck repairs, fuel, insurance, and all other overhead expenses. Overhead expenses of being an Owner Operator is a big undertaking financially. It takes truck drivers a lot of time to build up the capital to go into business for themselves unless they had previously saved the money they needed prior to coming into the industry. Make sure you do thorough research on this as well. A smart businessman or businesswoman can make a lot of money and have the luxury of independence.

Leasing Operator

Lease Operators are similar owner operators. They are their own business however, they pay a company a percentage of their salary to cover major expenses and insurance. For instance, they may choose to lease their truck onto a major carrier that has a split of 30 percent going to the major carrier and 70 percent going to Lease Operator to maintain their business expenses. So, if the lease operator drives and makes $6,000.00, the major carrier would take $1,800.00 to cover expenses like maintenance, truck tags, fuel, etc. Lease Operators still make more than the company driver but they still have some of the benefits that they pay for in their percentage that owner operators do not receive being independent. It is a great option if you do not want to take on the expense or the burden of starting your own trucking authority.

Fleet Owner

Fleet Owners are similar to Owner Operators in the sense that they are their own business entity and consume all the expenses of running the business. Fleet owners are generally a bit smaller in size than major carriers. Major carriers normally have hundreds of trucks on the road at one time whereas most small fleet owners have just a few trucks. A fleet owner can grow their fleet as large as they are comfortable with growing. With every truck comes its own set of expenses. So, for many fleet owners they never try to grow as large as a major carrier. They do enough to make the money they would like to. Fleet owners make great money because they have the ability to have more than one major asset on the road making them money. Again, this is an area I suggest highly researching because this can become a huge money maker for someone with ambition to have people working for them in the future.

Which is best?

After you get your CDL the sky is really the limit the trucking aspect of the transportation industry. The industry is flexible. You really have to figure out what you can handle at the moment when you start driving. Your finances play a major role in the decision of where to start off in this industry and how comfortable you are with driving. If you are starting out with little money, you may have to start with a major carrier and go through their CDL program to get your foot in the door. You will have to work for that company for a year unless you self-pay. But if you really think about it, that is really not bad considering for the first three months of the year contract you will be in training. If you have assets you could go and pay for school to get your license and maybe work locally until you have the option to become an owner operator. You can always stay a company driver for the benefits as well. Just remember when you have that CDL you can take many different paths and your potential is unlimited. By no means am I saying it will be easy but it is definitely worth doing your own homework on this and work the effort it takes to be in the trucking industry. No matter what you do you will have some obstacles but remember anything worth having is worth the effort.

8

Making Money as a Freight Dispatcher or Broker

Freight dispatching and freight brokering are similar in the sense that you are not required to have a physical truck to get started. Freight dispatching and freight brokering are extremely profitable business structures that you can do while you're still working a nine-to-five job. Simply use either one of these business types as and additional stream of income that you can choose to transition into a full-time business later.

Starting requirements for freight dispatching or brokering is: developing a business legal structure, secure an EIN (you can get this for free at www.irs.gov, have a business checking account, and a marketing plan. For many people, we already know some truck drivers personally. However, if you want to grow your business you need to be aware that you will have to connect with other truck drivers.

When it comes to freight dispatching independently you will have to learn through some form of training how to set up your business and what it takes to dispatch for owner-operators. You can find an online course or you can find in-person training to teach you how to start a dispatching service. When I started my business, I went through an online course because it was cheaper and easier for me to access the information immediately versus having to wait for someone to teach a seminar or course. If you do decide to go in person please understand that it will likely cost quite a bit more because you're having to pay for the instructor's time and materials that are provided. When choosing a course I would suggest selecting the learning method based on your learning style so you can maximize your learning experience and not waste your money. These courses and seminars are not hard to find however I do feel like you should do a significant amount of research before purchasing a course. I feel like I learned the basics of what I needed to do for my business through my training course. However, I do plan to create my training course to improve on what I felt like was missing from my training course. I felt like there was a lot of information left out and it could have been done a lot more thoroughly. A lot of the things that I have learned have been through trial and error. I highly recommend that before you decide to go the freight dispatching route that you find a good course or a good mentor in the industry already that you can work with.

How is freight dispatching so lucrative???

Freight dispatchers get paid based on the number of trucks that they are servicing. On average, most dispatchers charge a rate of 5-10% of the weekly total dispatches that they service to owner-operators. In a good economy and a thriving transportation market, each truck can earn up to $5,000 or more per week. This is all depending upon how hard the truck driver likes to run and if they are doing over the road driving. You will find that a lot of owner-operators prefer to stay close to home which allows them to be able to come home every other day or once a week. When you are dealing with an owner-operator that likes to stay regionally or close to home sometimes it can be hard to achieve larger amounts of income, but it also depends on how well the market is going.

As a good dispatcher, your goal is to plan the route in the most profitable way for your owner operator truck drivers to make the most money because you get paid based on what the routes they run throughout the week. If you are charging 10% of the loads for the week per truck and they're making $5,000 per week you are going to make $500 a week per truck. So, if you have a fleet of seven trucks you are making $3,500 per week as long as these trucks are grossing $5,000 per week. This is not hard to accomplish if you know what you are doing.

Freight brokering also requires you to have some initial training to help you understand how it works. It is a similar business set-up structure like dispatching, which is very simple. You can also find mini broker courses online to teach you how to go about getting into freight brokering.

Here is a simple explanation of how freight brokering works. Essentially the broker is the middleman between the manufacturer and the dispatcher or owner-operator. Freight brokers negotiate with companies and manufacturers to agree on a rate that they can get trucks to move their items.

To give you an idea of how they make money, let me give you an example. Let's say John decides to be a freight broker and he finds a manufacturer that will allow him to move 3 different trucks. John has negotiated to move all the freight for this company for $2,000. This manufacturer needs this freight moved every day to service its clients or manufacturers. So what John would do after he signs a contract with the manufacturer, he will upload all the information that he has on the company that he's trying to move for a lower amount than what he negotiated. So John would then put he is going to give a truck driver $1,500 to move this freight on to a digital load board. (A load board is a website where dispatchers and truck drivers go to find freight that brokers are trying to get moved.) Brokers go to these websites to find drivers for their manufacturers. After John posted this information on to a load board for that rate he will start getting several calls from dispatchers and truck drivers to negotiate to move that freight. The price that John negotiates with a dispatcher or truck is less than what he negotiated with the manufacturer so he can make his profit. So let us say John can negotiate a price of $1,700 for the three different trucks that he needs the freight moved. The difference between the price he negotiated with the manufacturer and the price that he got the truck driver to take is $300. John would then have made a profit of

$900 and less than 2 hours. If he is doing the same thing 5 days a week he profits $4,500 a week if he negotiates it at that rate. Sometimes he can find truck drivers to take lower pay and sometimes he will find truck drivers that will not want to take anything less than what he has negotiated with the manufacturer.

The hardest thing about starting as a freight broker is that you have to reach out to several hundred manufacturers before you get one to work with you. But if you are consistent and willing to do the work it will pay off big-time. Most freight brokers or broker agents make six figures easily after they have secured a client.

In this industry, you will hear people refer to broker agents and freight brokers. The difference between the two is that a freight broker likely has its independent brokerage to obtain a brokerage; you will need to have the same business structure but you will also be required to purchase a surety bond. A surety bond ensures the safety of the freight that is being moved. It protects the freight broker, the freight brokerage, and manufacturer in the case that anything were to happen in the process of the freight being transported. The cost of surety bonds are based on your credit, and it operates similar to purchasing insurance for your home or car. Surety bonds can be as low as $1,500 and go as high as $5,000 on average, and the rate will vary depending on the company and your credit rating.

Freight agents do exactly what a freight broker does however, they do not have their own brokerage. They work under another company with a brokerage license and give the company they work for a small percentage of their profit to work under the company's broker license. A broker agent will pay anywhere from 50% to 25% of their profits to the company that they are working for.

This is just a basic overview of freight brokering and freight dispatching. It is much more detailed than what I have provided, but I wanted to provide a basic definition and introduction on how freight brokers and dispatchers make money without having trucks. It takes a lot of work to run these types of businesses as well but once you get the hang of it it becomes easier. Obtaining contracted carriers for owner-operators can be difficult at times for dispatchers just as securing a manufacturer or a client for a freight broker can be difficult when starting. For any business, you choose to run, I highly suggest you getting a mentor. Mentorship can be everything you need to be successful!

9

Making Money as a Small Fleet Owner

You have options to become a fleet owner. Making money as a fleet owner is very lucrative, however is not for everyone. Fleet ownership requires a great deal of business savvy and a lot of responsibility. You are responsible for any and everything that goes on with the tractor-trailers and whatever trailers that you have attached to those tractor-trailer trucks maintenance, you are responsible for your employees' income, and you are also responsible for any other overhead cause that comes along with maintaining a fleet. You are responsible for your employees and their benefits.

When running/operating a truck, you have to factor in how much it costs just for the fuel which is going to cost is weekly. You also have to make sure you have enough money and reserve for anything that could happen to your truck that will require a significant amount of maintenance. You also have to be mindful of the fact that you have to deal with the personalities of the drivers. And you also have to be sure that the correct insurance is obtained to cover these types of trucks, which can be quite expensive. There's a lot that comes with this but there are two ways that you can become a fleet owner if this is what you truly desire.

Operating Your Authority

Starting and maintaining your own Trucking Authority is extremely costly and expensive for the initial start. You have to buy your truck, of course, but you also have several other expenses that you may have not considered. Now all of the things I am about to tell you, some of it can be done through leveraging credit. You need to make sure that you have enough cash reserves to cover any major expenses that can come up. Insurance does not cover everything and credit cards do not cover everything. You need cold hard cash to support your business as well!

The requirements that it takes to start up your own Trucking Authority can cost you on the low end of $20,000.00, not including the truck. Now there are multiple options when building your fleet but I would say make sure you purchase **reliable** trucks. I would also make sure that of course, you have a good team if you have multiple people involved in your business. And just understand that this industry is volatile. You have to realize that there are going to be some very great moments in this industry where you will be making lots of money and there are going to be times where your company may not bring in as much money because the rates are low for the trade.

Everyone decides to build their fleet differently and here is a way that I think is a good way to go about it. But again, you have to move according to what your needs are. As a start-up, I would recommend buying used equipment to reduce the startup cost being so high. Also keep in mind, there is a lot of paperwork and documentation that will be required. Some of the fees that will be associated: auto and liability insurance, registration with Department of Transportation, securing a Motor Carrier number, getting tags for your trucks, etc. The list goes on and fees differ from state to state. These are not exact numbers, only estimates, but expect to spend a minimum of

$20,000.00 to have the correct documentation and legal things taken care of. Also, don't forget there will be costs for setting up your back office to run the business.

When it comes to purchasing a new truck I would do a lot of research and I do mean a lot of research! Look up various ways you can purchase your truck or trucks, especially if you're coming out of pocket to start this venture and you don't have a significant amount of funding to work with. I would suggest finding someone to teach you what it is that you need to be looking for in your trucks and your trailers. I would also consider reaching out to a truck driver you may know I'm sure you or someone close to you know someone that drives trucks as their job and can tell you more about how they function. If these methods don't work for you, I would recommend contacting a reputable diesel mechanic or one that you trust to be very honest with you. I also suggest maybe asking them in their off time if they would be willing to go with you to the dealership to test some of these trucks out and to make sure they are okay under the hood. You can also get a truck driver when you go pick up these trucks to sit in the front seat to make sure everything looks okay especially if you're not going to be the person driving.

You also want to make sure you do your research on the functionality of each make and model of the trucks. There are tons of reviews online about different types of trucks and the issues that some of them may have. I know certain brands some truck drivers refuse to drive because they've had several issues with that particular brand of trucks. There are also certain engine types that you don't want to have in your truck because they're costly to maintain. I would thoroughly research and understand the major problems that you will find in different brands of trucks. There is a wealth of knowledge throughout the internet if you take the time to look through them. I am not going to tell you which track is best for you and your situation because I don't completely know your situation but I do know that some trucks are not great for over-the-road Trucking but they might be great for local driving. And you will see this vice versa as well.

Lease Operator/ Lease-ON Fleet Owners

You can become a fleet owner by going through the route of being an owner-operator. You may want to purchase a truck through a major carrier that has a financing program. A lot of people go this route first before taking the Trucking Authority route because they want to see if they like being an owner-operator first before starting their fleet. The second way to become a lease operator fleet owner is by purchasing a truck and allowing major carriers such as Landstar or Schneider to use your truck under their motor carrier number and Department of Transportation number and you run freight for their company.

When leasing with a company via the owner-operator route in which you purchase the truck through the major carrier, and drive for them and pay the monthly truck note you need to pay attention to the terms of your lease agreement. This also includes ANY agreement. Make sure you know the ins and out of what the terms are in the contracts. A lot of people get caught up at the point of signing a lease to purchase a truck. All lease agreements are not the same and all leases are not good leases.

The concept of leasing a truck is very similar to how you at least a car. You agree to make payments on the truck for several months, you agree to how many miles you drive before you pay a penalty, and you agree to maintain the truck and keep it in the same or is a new condition as possible. Most major carriers sell these trucks if they are turned in by the owner-operator at the end of the lease term to be resold. I would not get caught up in having a new truck every year because in these types of agreements you will always be stuck making payments the truck lease. Unless being a lifelong lease operator through a major carrier is a part of your business model I would not trade in my truck unless there were issues that you saw getting ready to happen with the truck.

You can also be at lease operator fleet on her by purchasing a truck outside of one of the major carrier companies and having them use that same truck to run the same freight. What makes this different is that you own your truck without being required to turn it in after the end of the lease. You could buy a used truck and then turn around sign it on to one of those major carriers and make the same money with lower overhead than someone who has the newest tractor-trailer from a dealership and make a larger profit margin for your stuff. A lot of people are investing this way in the trucking industry.

Think about it, you could buy a used truck that is in really good shape and sign it on to one of these companies. You could hire a driver for each truck that you have leased onto a major carrier. Right now I would say the industry average for a driver is anywhere from $0.45 to $0.55 per mile on average. The driver makes money per mile based on experience so this can be subjective from company to company and from division to division.   Before sharing an example, I'm going to discuss a job that pays $0.50 per mile. Now each carrier has different benefits, costs, and requirements to do business with this driver. Let's say we have a company named Snoopy & Friends Transportation. This company allows you to earn 70% of your gross settlements or weekly earnings per truck. The 30% the carrier takes will cover your insurance, your tags, load boards, and a few other things that are included in your package.

Now let's say your driver does 3,000 miles every week and there is a gross of $5,500 for weight in your truck. Because your driver makes $0.50 per mile his gross for that week would be $1,500. Let's say he did $1,000 and fuel as a business owner you put $750 into an escrow account for maintenance, and you put aside an additional $500 just in case there are any additional expenses. That leaves you with $1,750 for that week in profit for your business. And you multiply that by 52 weeks out of the year it will leave you with $91,000 profit. Now granted every week your driver will not be running and every week your truck will not be running but this just shows you the potential profit you can have if you were to have someone working for you. my numbers are not exact so please do not take this to heart but it does get across the point that you can invest in trucking and not ever leave home. Through my example, I hope you're able to at least get an idea of what your potential earnings *could* be. And also want you to consider what it would bring in to have multiple trucks running under one of these major carriers.

What will make the real-life experience different than the example that I showed you is that there are several factors to consider when calculating numbers. You have to consider the age of the truck and the mileage that's on the truck because it makes a difference in how much maintenance is required and maintaining the truck. if you have an independent dispatcher you also have to factor in their fees into your cost of maintaining your trucks. and you also have to consider the fact that some of your drivers will request home time from off the road a few weeks out of the year. It depends on what they have going on at home and if they have a family.

One Last Thing

There are pros and cons to having your own independent Trucking Authority. and there's pros and cons to being a leaseholder. When considering to go either route just look at when it comes to dollars and cents how much are you going to profit. I've seen some fleet owners make more money being at lease on fleet owners than a person who owns their own Trucking Authority. You need to make a decision on what's right for you and go from there. The good part about being a Trucking Authority is that you don't have to answer to anybody however you are responsible for everything. The benefit of being a lease on fleet owner is that some of the responsibilities are shared with the company that you are a carrier for and it's not just you.

Make sure when you decide to invest in being a fleet owner by starting your own Trucking Authority that you have a decent mentor. You can find mentors for a nominal fee I'm depending on where you find your mentor. or you could get someone that you have encountered through networking to see if they would be willing to answer questions or mentor you. Mentorship is just another tool that would be to your advantage to maintain stability in this industry. I would make sure when choosing a mentor that the mentor is very knowledgeable and has been through a few things in this industry to make them read in this industry. Even if they've had significant losses and have made many mistakes you can learn a lot from their mistakes if you sit back and listen to the things that they have done.

Lastly, coming to this industry with a plan. The plan can change daily or yearly but have a plan. and don't limit yourself in learning other ways to make money in this industry. Once you get in this industry and begin to learn more and more you will see more opportunities to make money. Also, don't be limited to learning just from one perspective. Because from each person that you speak with you will begin to learn different ways of doing things that may benefit your business. And be mindful of who you're seeking advice from. make sure the people that are helping you are really in your corner rooting for you. Some people give bad advice with good intentions. And some people advise with bad intentions.

10
Conclusion

My goal with this book was to help you learn and understand that there are many ways that you can make money in this industry without having to have a brick-and-mortar established. In this book, I hope I have planted the seed that will lead you to new opportunities. Just as with any other business, the transportation industry has a lot to offer and there are many ways that you can be a part of this industry. It can be extremely lucrative and rewarding at the same time.

As I have mentioned before within the book I highly recommend you doing an ample amount of research and figuring out what path is best for you. for many people, starting a business can be hard and it is great to have a mentor for a consultant to talk to regarding how to grow your business. If you are smart about the path you decide to take you can save a lot of money and put together a strategy. but the best way to learn more about this industry is to eventually get out and do something in it. Learning through trial and error will teach you more than hearing someone else talk about the business. To gain real success in this business it will take a hustler mindset and a willingness to keep going even when you feel like you cannot. The goal in life is to have multiple streams of income to create generational wealth.

If you ever have any questions or would like to book me for speaking engagements, please feel free to reach out to me via social media and I will try to get back to you if I can. You can find me on Facebook and Instagram @southernbellelogistics. I am a pretty straightforward person, and even if I cannot help you I will let you know. I will try my best to point you in the right direction at least to get your question answered or finding someone that can help you further. Please do not be upset if your question requires a consultation because I do charge those fees. Some of you will ask me harder questions that require more time to have them answered. And if you decide to get into the trucking business please let me know! I love the support and to see other businesses grow. I have more content coming so please be on the lookout.

Common Terminology

Back Haul: The trip back to the point of origin after delivery.

Bill of Lading: A document issued by a carrier to a shipper, signed by the captain, agent, or owner of a vessel, furnishing written evidence regarding receipt of freight, the conditions on which transportation is made and the date to deliver goods at the prescribed port of destination to the lawful holder of the bill of lading.

Billed Weight: The designated weight is shown on an invoice and/or waybill used to calculate freight charges.

Bobtail: Tractor operating without a trailer, also known as a deadhead.

Breakbulk: Unpacking or disassembling a portion or all contents of a consolidated shipment for consignment or delivery.

Bridge Formula: A bridge protection formula used by federal and state governments to regulate the amount of weight that can be put on each of a vehicle's axles, and how far apart the axles must be.

Bulk Cargo: Cargo stowed loosely in the hold of a ship and is not enclosed in a shipper container or box. Examples include oil, ore, grain or coal.

Cargo: The goods or merchandise transported by airplane, ship or vehicle.

Cargo Manifest: A list of cargo being transported or warehoused, without listing the applicable charges.

Carrier: Any individual or firm who, through a contract of carriage, undertakes to perform or procure the performance of carriage by rail, road, sea, air, inland waterway, or by a combination of modes.

Common Carrier: A trucking company that will haul freight to anyone. This is different than other companies that only haul to private or dedicated customers.

Contract Carrier: A trucking company that hauls freight to less customers under a trucking contract.

Deadhead: A truck with no cargo.

Dimensional Weight: A calculated weight based on a minimum density requirement. Density is the weight per cubic foot of a shipment of cargo. It is computed by dividing the shipment volume by the minimum density requirement. The dimensional weight rule was developed to ensure fair compensation to low-density shipments under which the transportation charges are based on a cubic dimensional weight rather than upon actual weight.

Doubles: A combination of a truck and two trailers.

Drayage: Carrying freight a short distance as part of a longer trip. For example, a tractor picking up freight from a rail yard and carrying it 50 miles to its final destination.

Durable Goods Product: that is not consumed through use, such as automobiles, furniture, computers, and machinery.

E-Log: A computer system that keeps track of a truck driver's miles and service. When using an E-log, carries will have instant access to their driver's logs. This allows carriers to improve scheduling drivers.

Entry: Documentation of the kinds, quantities, and values of goods imported together with duties due and declared before a customs officer. It is required to secure the release from customs custody.

ETA: Acronym for Estimated Time of Arrival of a carrier.

FTL: Full-Truck-Load: drayage company is moving a full container from one destination to the next.

Hours of Service (HOS): Federal regulations that govern the number of hours a truck driver may operate a commercial vehicle.

Logbook: Record of mileage, driving hours, and rest time that complies with federal Hours of Service regulations. A logbook can either be paper or electronic.

Long-Haul: A long-distance drive that is usually several hundred miles or more. This is also called Over-the-Road (OTR).

LTL: Less-Than-Truckload. Carrying less cargo than a full truckload weight for a customer. This includes shipping one package or half of a truckload.

OTR: Over-the-Road. Long-haul trucking, as opposed to local or regional.

Qualcomm: Carriers use wireless communication that uses GPS, text messaging and email. Qualcomm allows the trucking company to keep track of its drivers along with the status of deliveries and weather.

Relay – Two drivers start out in two different origin points several hours apart with loaded trucks. They meet in the middle, exchange cargo and return to their points of origin.

Reefer – Refrigerated trailer that has a cooling unit in the front and insulated walls. It's like driving a giant freezer. These are usually used for perishable food items.

Team: Two drivers who alternate driving and sleeping schedules to make delivery as fast as possible while staying within federal Hours of Service guidelines.

TL: Truckload – Fully-loaded truck (flatbed or box)

TL Carrier: A trucking company that hauls a single freight on one truckload.

Popular CDL Schools Worth Mentioning

* Crete Carrier-http://www.cretecarrier.com
* Prime, Inc.-http://www.primeinc.com
* Swift Transportation-http://www.swiftrans.com
* KLLM Transport Services-http://www.kllm.com
* Maverick Transportation (one of the best paying for student drivers)-http://www.maverickusa.com
* Schneider-http://www.schneider.com
* U.S. Express-https://www.usxjobs.com/
* Steven Transport-https://www.stevenstransport.com/
* CRST Transport-https://www.crst.com/
* Melton Trucking-https://meltontruck.com
* J.B. Hunt-https://www.jbhunt.com/

* TMC Transportation-

https://www.tmctrans.com/

* Knight Transportation-

https://driveknight.com/

* CR England-https://www.drivecre.com

* FFE Transportation-

https://www.ffeinc.com/

* Pam Transport-

https://pamtransport.greatcdltraining.com/

* Stein Beer (distribution company that trains
their drivers)-

https://www.steinbeer.com/now-hiring-class-
a-cdl-delivery-drivers-1000-sign-on-bonus-w-
paid-cdl-training/

* Roehl Transportation-

https://www.roehl.jobs/driving-jobs/cdl-
truck-driving-schools

* TMC Trans-https://www.roehl.jobs/driving-
jobs/cdl-truck-driving-schools

* Wil-Trans-http://www.wil-
trans.com/careers/training/

Types of Trucks Commonly Used

FLATBED

DRY VAN

REFRIGERATED TRUCK (a.k.a. REEFER)

STEPDECK TRAILER/LOW-BOY

REMOVABLE GOOSENECK

FLATBED TRUCK W/SIDE KIT

RNG TRUCK

CONESTOGA TRUCK

MULTI-CAR TRAILER

ABOUT THE AUTHOR

I never thought I would ever become an author. It is funny how God and life experiences kind of have a way of changing your plans and everything you thought you would be. I'm originally from Clarksville, Tennessee. I was brought up in a single-parent household and from a very large family. Although I was raised as the only child, I had plenty of cousins and friends who kept me entertained. Life has never really been easy for me but I pride myself on overcoming the stereotypes of a child that is raised by a single parent.

I think the one thing that always stuck with me growing up is how my parents would encourage me to be the best version of myself. When I was in elementary school I was told by a relative that I would not do well because I was raised in a single-parent household. And there's always been something inside of me when someone told me I could not do something it just ignited a fire in my stomach to make me want to accomplish everything that they said I cannot accomplish. With that passion to prove myself that I could do anything that I set my mind to improve everyone that's ever doubted me I focused on getting the best grades that I can get and completing college outside of my hometown. Clarksville, Tennessee will always be home however, I knew from the time I was in elementary school that I would not live my life there as an adult.

I started my education at Middle Tennessee State University and attended there for about two years until I party my way out of school. I am normally was a pretty good student however when you get that bit of freedom of being on your own it is always difficult to balance the new life that I was trying to live. In 2010 I moved to Los Angeles, California and a lot of things began to happen that were unexpected. Living in Los Angeles taught me a lot and while I was there I decided to work for the State of California. Working for them required me to relocate to the Sacramento area. I feel like during this time of my life is where I had to be the most adult and make a lot of decisions that would change my life.

While I was in Northern California, I learned a lot of hard lessons and I also got back on track and completed my education as well as started doing well in my career. Unfortunately, towards the end of 2016 and through most of 2017 a lot of tragedies happened within the family that made me make the decision to move to Houston, Texas. I needed to be in between both sides of my family in which they both still lived in Tennessee and in California.

I have a love-hate feeling about Houston. I never thought I would be an entrepreneur until I had moved to Houston. Moving to Houston was one of the most difficult things I have ever had to do. Houston has taught me to create your own platform to be successful. I never had a hard time getting a job until I move to Houston. This city is more about who you know versus what you know. I had several years of experience in the industry that I was in and was well-qualified or overqualified for most of the positions I was applying for. Most jobs that I could get were either contract or temp work. Which was not stable and I know I had more to offer than just that. Through my frustration, I decided to start my own business. I actually started two other businesses before I started my trucking business. and I'm happy I made the decision to go with trucking and plan to add more services soon to my business. I have learned so much over the last year-and-a-half on my entrepreneurship journey. I hope that through my book that I'm able to help people understand that anybody can do what it is that they set out to do. And if they're interested in getting into this business that it is easier than you think. It just takes a lot of research and hard work.

Make Sure You Follow Cheyara Collier on Social Media!

Linkedin: Cheyara Collier

Facebook: @southernbellelogistics

Instagram: @southernbellelogistics

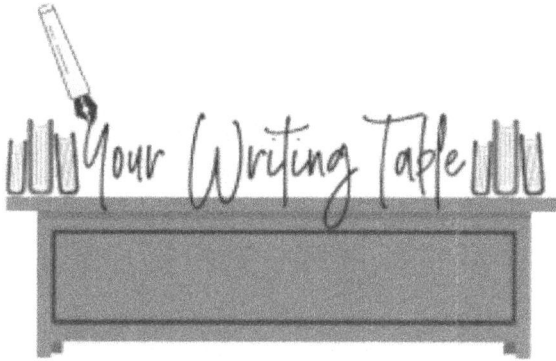

Your Writing Table

Interested in writing your own book or need some editing assistance with a current project? Please contact us for details!

Packages & pricing are available for ALL budgets!

YOUR book, YOUR way!

Call or email today for a consultation!

chelsia@chelsiamccoy.com or by

phone: (832)422-6455

Making YOUR literary dreams come true!

www.ingramcontent.com/pod-product-compliance
Lightning Source LLC
Chambersburg PA
CBHW062035200326
41519CB00017B/5047